FREE VERSE

Free Verse

POEMS FOR RICHARD PRICE

EDITED BY

DAMIAN WALFORD DAVIES
& KEVIN MILLS

SEREN

Seren is the book imprint of
Poetry Wales Press Ltd.
Suite 6, 4 Derwen Road, Bridgend, Wales, CF31 1LH
www.serenbooks.com
facebook.com/SerenBooks
twitter@SerenBooks

www.serenbooks.com
facebook.com/SerenBooks
twitter@SerenBooks

Introduction © Damian Walford Davies, 2023
Poems © individual authors

ISBN: 978-1-78172-746-1

A CIP record for this title is available from the British Library.

Cover painting: *Richard Price* by Kevin Sinnott.
Photograph: Chris Lloyd.

Printed in Bembo by 4Edge Ltd, Hockley.

Contents

Introduction: Richard Price Redivivus

On the cover of this collection, the interlinked Welsh, European and transatlantic worlds of Dr Richard Price (1723–91) – easily the most distinguished Welsh thinker lost to popular consciousness – are assembled in Kevin Sinnott's painting into a kinetic and visionary scene. Something of the paradox of Price is captured in the contrast between the swirling, surging, pitching and stabbing international action and verbal flow on the one hand and on the other, the apparent calm of the seated, bewigged figure in the sober black of the eighteenth-century Dissenting minister (the fashions Price chose were apparently a good generation behind the times).

Price's quill is poised next to the whitewashed gable end of his birth-place – Tynton Farm, Llangeinor in the Garw Valley, south Wales. Below, we watch his younger self being led along a track that, geographically at least, would take him no further than London, where as a Dissenter barred from public office by the penal laws enshrined in the Test Acts, he spent his life ministering to intellectually vibrant nonconformist congregations in Newington Green and Hackney. His was, in many ways, a modest and circumscribed life. Yet his writings on civil, political and religious liberty in support of the revolutions in America and France – and his consistent advocacy of reform, toleration and freedom of inquiry at home – would make him an international celebrity, as well as the subject of lampoons and death threats. During his lifetime he would have heard himself referred to by his admirers as the 'Friend of the Universe'; his detractors chose to call him 'the calculating divine' and 'the Arch-devil'.[1]

At the bottom right of Sinnott's painting are two figures dressed as Native Americans, one carrying a chest of tea. These are the (white) members of the 'Sons of Liberty' paramilitary group who in 1773 appropriated the dress of the Mohawk nation to stage the Boston Tea Party, in which tea carried by British East India Company ships was dumped into Boston harbour in protest at the British Government's colonial trade and tax policies. Over Price's right shoulder, like a phantom battle in the sky, a scene from the American Revolutionary War (1775–83) is playing out: General Washington, mounted and sporting a tricorne hat, leads his troops under the American flag against British redcoats, one of whom has raised his Brown Bess rifle, ready to strike with his bayonet. Beneath, a drummer boy seems almost to be shielding Tynton from violence.

Price, around whom these actions rage, was one of the principal form-ulators of the intellectual case for America's existence. As D. O. Thomas reminds us, up to the outbreak of the American War of Independence,

Price's fame and influence were confined to 'the relatively small circle of those who read his writings on moral philosophy, theology, probability theory, assurance and the nation's finances'.[2] Publications such as *A Review of the Principal Questions and Difficulties in Morals* (1758), *Observations on Reversionary Payments* (1771) and *An Essay on the Population* (1780), while trailblazing in their respective fields, were not the basis of what his reactionary critics would term his 'Gunpowder Legacy' (though it is important to emphasise the consistency, connection and cumulative force that bind together the range of analyses and arguments across all his works).[3] His reputation as both a visionary thinker and a practical adviser in the Atlantic intellectual world was formed by the pamphlets that defended the rebels and articulated the moral and political principles on which the nascent and fledgling republic of America claimed self-determination — *Observations on the Nature of Civil Liberty* (1776), which swiftly sold sixty thousand copies, and *Observations on the Importance of the American Revolution* (1784). For the founding feminist philosopher Mary Wollstonecraft, who had moved to Newington Green in 1784 to set up a school, Price was quite simply 'Le Sage', whose unassuming lifestyle, conscientiousness as a preacher and warm mentorship belied the global reach and heady impact of his thought.[4]

Alongside Thomas Paine's *Common Sense* (1776), Price's pamphlets offered nothing less than a moral, political and legislative blueprint for a new nation. His emphasis was on financial realities and transatlantic logistics, not simply the imperatives of abstract rights; for Price, the American Revolutionary War was one that the 'parent' state of Britain neither should nor could have won: 'No wonder . . . that they have turned upon us, and obliged us to remember they are not children', he wrote.[5] Congress offered him American citizenship in 1778 — in essence an invitation to emigrate that he declined; three years later, he and George Washington received the degree of Doctor of Laws from Yale University. Price was far-sighted, knowing how carefully the young nation needed to guard against abuses of power. Deprecating slavery, to which America was still wedded, in the strongest terms — 'It is a traffic which . . . is shocking to humanity, cruel, wicked and diabolical'[6] — he continued to give friends and correspondents such as the Founding Fathers George Washington, John Adams, Benjamin Franklin, Thomas Jefferson and John Jay practical, logistical and financial, as well as moral and political, advice. His analyses were always future-focused; the new polity needed to be future-proof.

Returning to Sinnott's painting: over Price's left shoulder, the female carrying the French *tricolore* is clearly the allegorical figure in Eugène Delacroix's famous *Liberty Leading the People* (1830) which commemorates not the French Revolution of 1789, which Price famously welcomed as a world-altering event that was a staging-post on the road to human perfectibility, but the 'July Revolution' of 1830. This section of Sinnott's canvas is therefore one of dislocating juxtapositions and timeslips: Liberty advances over the (later) Parisian barricades, a young supporter in tow, next to a vertiginous guillotine that symbolises the passage of the Revolution of 1789 from its constitutional beginnings through the September Massacres of 1792 and the obscene violence, retribution and paranoia of Robespierre's Reign of Terror of 1793–4 to France's later imperial expansionism under Napoleon. The welcome Price gave at the end of 1789 to the early stages of the Revolution was a spark that ignited the dynamic pamphlet war known as the Revolution Controversy – the last great expansive discussion of natural and civil rights and political representation in Britain.

Price, we must remember, had a day job. His lifelong public platform was the pulpit as well as the pamphlet. This was as much his debating arena as the burgeoning culture of print media or 'fuggy', smoke-filled sociable spaces such as St Paul's Coffee House where, with fellow intellectuals such as Franklin and the Unitarian chemist and philosopher Joseph Priestley, he attended the Club of Honest Whigs.[7] When the Bastille fell on 14 July 1789 and a new constitutional arrangement was brokered, Price took the opportunity to hail the arrival of an event whose meaning and ramifications he recognised as both spiritual and material-political. He did so on 4 November 1789 in a sermon from the pulpit at the Old Jewry meeting house; the address was published immediately as *A Discourse on the Love of our Country* (1789). Lyndall Gordon notes that Price had throughout his life 'preached liberty as part of a programme of moral perfection'; he had also unswervingly rehearsed the maxim that political authority ultimately resides with the people.[8] The ostensible occasion for the autumn 1789 sermon was the commemoration of the so-called 'Glorious Revolution' of 1688–9 that saw the exile of the Catholic James II, the accession of William and Mary and the establishment of parliamentary sovereignty as part of a Protestant constitutional monarchy. Price – always a connecting thinker – links three revolutions in a continuum of improvement and emancipation:

> What an eventful period this is! I am thankful that I have lived to see it, and I could almost say, *Lord, now lettest thou thy servant depart in peace, for mine eyes have seen they salvation* . . . After sharing in the benefits of one Revolution, I have been spared to be a witness to two other Revolutions, both glorious . . . Be encouraged, all ye

friends of freedom, and writers in its defence! . . . Behold, the light you have struck out, after setting America free, reflected to France, and there kindled into a blaze that lays despotism in ashes, and warms and illuminates Europe![9]

Peppered through the published pamphlet are remarks on King George III's constitutional status as 'no more than the first servant of the public' and on the right 'to chuse our own governors; to cashier them for misconduct; and to frame a government for ourselves'.[10] Price must have known that these were rhetorical, tendentious and inflammatory political short-cuts. It was such statements from the pulpit that the Anglo-Irish statesman and philosopher Edmund Burke (a one-time supporter of the rights of the American colonists) seized on in his great defence of precedent, 'body and stock of inheritance' and organic conservatism, *Reflections on the Revolution in France* (1790).[11] His jumping-off point was an attack on Price's political 'porridge' and 'harangue'. For Burke, Price's principles harked back not to the Glorious Revolution's bloodless coup but to the king-killing terror of the English Civil War of the 1640s. Burke's Price is 'a man much connected with literary caballers, and intriguing philosophers; with political theologians, and theological politicians, both at home and abroad'.[12] The descent of the French Revolution, post-1792, into blood and terror gave Burke's *Reflections*, as Jonathan Wordsworth remarks, 'a somewhat spurious air of prophecy'.[13] Though Price technically remained a constitutionalist throughout his life, contemporaries were right to identify the radicalism (not just reformism) that underpinned his writings. Learning of the last illnesses of both the Comte de Mirabeau (an early leader of the French Revolution and one of Price's high-profile correspondents) and of Price himself, Horace Walpole wrote to a friend: 'Dr Price is dying also — fortunate omens for those who hope to die in their beds too'.[14] The portrait of Price as a lean, treasonous, black-clad Welsh wizard stirring jacobinical porridge in the cauldron of radicalism is both absurd and instructive.

Price, with Burke as it were on his back, takes centre stage in Sinnott's painting. The artist renders Price as younger than the eminent but plain preacher we see in the portrait painted in 1784 by Benjamin West, in which he wears a wig that sits on him like outsized earmuffs. Price's head is turned to his left; seemingly unphased, he is listening to Burke's hissed or muttered strictures, and offering ripostes. In Sinnott's preparatory painting, there was no Burke behind Price. But in a nod to the famous 1790 caricature by James Gillray, *Smelling out a Rat; or The Atheistical-revolutionist Disturbed in his Midnight 'Calculations'* (in which Burke's long nose extends like a surveillance instrument into philosopher-mathematician Price's study, where he is busy penning seditious pamphlets beneath a picture of the execution of Charles I), Sinnott brings a prying Burke into the global historical drama of the finished picture. The two antagonists trade serpentine lines of speech: against Burke's classic formulation 'The best way to preserve the peace and unity of a nation is by the principle of hereditary succession', Price offers: 'Every community has the right to govern itself' and (in French and English) 'Nothing is more necessary than the establishment of a system of education'. The latter statement, from *Observations on the Importance of the American Revolution*, seems also to channel the focus and spirit of Wollstonecraft, who was the first to defend Price publicly against Burke's attacks in her *Vindication of the Rights of Men* (1790). In an act of connected thinking characteristic of her mentor, the non-compartmentalising Price, her arguments in that salvo were expanded two years later in *A Vindication of the Rights of Woman* to encompass the education, and disenfranchisement, of women. (It is tempting to think that Price learned as much from Wollstonecraft as she learned from him.) Further, streaming from Price's quill like tickertape in Sinnott's image are some of the core principles that Price articulated in multiple sermons and pamphlets and which were formulated by others, the world over, as rallying cries and political avowals: 'No taxation without representation' and 'All men are created equal'. Here also are some of his own (in)famous pronouncements: 'Tremble all ye oppressors of the world!'.

The apparent anachronisms in Sinnott's painting work in interesting ways. The reference to the *next* French Revolution of 1830 embodied in Delacroix's female Liberty emphasises a nineteenth-century Pricean legacy of libertarianism and radicalism (undeniable, despite the long eclipse his name and reputation suffered after his death). At the same time, the image of the guillotine – the instrument of the French Terror – offers a challenge to Price and to our understanding of him. As Jonathan Wordsworth puts it pithily: 'Dying in 1791, [Price] was never forced, as were . . . others, to redefine his expectations'.[15]

And then there is the question of Wales. As Paul Frame and Geoffrey W. Powell note, Price 'makes very little of his Welshness in his own writings'.[16] The visibility Sinnott gives on his canvas to Tynton and Llangeinor raises the interesting question of the Welsh theological, political and cultural genetics of Price's thought. As noted earlier, in the painting we see his younger self, laden with books, being led out by a female figure (in 'traditional' Welsh costume that is in fact a confection of a later period of nation-building). This is, I suggest, just as allegorical an entity as Delacroix's Lady Liberty. As well as being Catherine, Richard's mother, delivering her (probably Welsh-speaking) son into the charge of various tutors, this is Lady Wales, delivering the young Richard Price onto a global anglophone stage. We know that Price roundly rejected the doctrine of predestination that characterised his father's Calvinism, emphasising rather an individual's agency as an autonomous actor with moral obligations. Those who posit a kind of Welsh pulpit *hwyl* behind a published performance such as *A Discourse on the Love of our Country* probably fly in the face of the facts: contemporary evidence such as that of the American visitor, Abigail Adams, who attended Price's sermons at the Gravel Pit, Hackney alongside her husband, identifies a low-key sincerity rather than a dramatic expressiveness as Price's pulpit mode: 'I revered the Character and Loved the Man. Tho far from being an orator, his words came from the Heart and reached the Heart'.[17]

Price's attachments (and obligations) were not to 'the soil or the spot of earth on which we happen to have been born, not the forests and fields, but that community of which we are members; or that body of companions and friends and kindred who are associated with us under the same constitution of government, protected by the same laws, and bound together by the same civil polity', as he notes in *A Discourse*.[18] Surely Price had in mind the specific 'forests and fields' of the Garw Valley when he wrote this. In other words, his was a non-place-based, civil, civic, non-sectarian identity. As Frame and Powell suggest, however, it is possible that his experience as a London Welshman may have informed a sense of belonging and a spirit of enquiry that transcended boundaries and valorised connection rather than cultural difference.[19]

That Price requires an introduction in 2023 – the tercentenary of his birth – is regrettable but explicable. Frame notes that 'Various factors have contributed to the forgetting of Richard Price'.[20] On his death he had a global profile and was fêted by the legislatures of America and France, though not by that of his native country. The impact of verbal and visual political lampoons of the 1790s; the loud and seemingly oracular voice of Burke, who popularised an image of Price as an armchair abstract theorist and metaphysical speculator; the irrefutable utopianism and long-since-unfashionable millenarian faith that characterised Price's thought; the driving underground of the reform movement in Britain after 1795 by William Pitt's 'Gagging Acts' and the government's system of spies and informers; the restoration of European monarchies post-Waterloo; and the crucial fact that Price's works were not republished in the decades following his death: all these conspire to render Price a casualty of cultural and political amnesia.

And yet Price's works and example have much to offer Wales and the world at a time of war in Europe, rising social inequality, forced migration and human displacement, post-pandemic inflationary crisis, new imperialisms, divisive populism, deeply entrenched racism, venality in public life and the existential threat of the climate emergency. The thinker who posited an early form of NATO and the United Nations, objected to war as hateful, asked his congregation and his readers to keep 'a jealous eye on [those] to whom they have committed the trust of government, and to resist as soon as they think oppression is beginning',[21] doggedly emphasised interpersonal moral obligations and the worth and sanctity of each human life and drummed the right of a community to self-determination would no doubt confront the above challenges (and opportunities) by marshalling practical solutions alongside core principles.

The poems commissioned for this volume explore Price's contemporary resonance by both channelling and challenging his legacy. Engaging with his work, life and afterlife, sixteen poets reflect on the various ways in which, in a 'world of hierarchies', and 'despite the fisting, thrusting, dumbing crush of it all', 'Price finds his way into [the] heart' (in the words of Mab Jones and Angela Graham). The volume offers imaginative access to and contemporary takes on Price the mathematician, actuarial scientist, demographer, Arian minister, political and probability theorist, theologian, friend, son, brother, mentor and sea bather. This is not hagiography or hero-worship. Alongside the directness of their decolonising enquiry, the poems' obliqueness, irony and puns test the relevance of Price's example in 2023, just as they test the 'account', 'testimonies', 'probabilities' and 'truth' of the contemporary world against Price's own positions. Importantly, the emotional and psychological geographies and micro- and macro-histories that these poems map through a Pricean lens are, like Price's own vision and Sinnott's painting, global and transhistorical: we move from Porthcawl to Iraq, Llangeinor to Michigan, Welsh moorland to Dhaka's 'subtropical afternoon'.

It would be neither opportunistic nor insensitive to claim that Richard Price might serve us well as one of the presiding spirits of a post-devolution, post-Brexit, post-pandemic, post-Trump, post-Black Lives Matter, post-#MeToo Wales in a burning world. The man whose avowed aim was to 'make the world free and happy'[22] deserves to reemerge forcefully into our public and political consciousness as one of the compasses by which we might navigate our stewardship of place, resources, democratic polity and language for future generations and for a cooler world.

A parting glimpse of Price at a meeting of the Club of Honest Whigs offers both a revealing picture of the physical manifestations of the workings of Price's intellect and fervour and a prompt for creative, Price-inspired thought and action for the future. Paul Frame records that 'in the heat of [political] debate, Price "turned his wig round on his head, twisted one leg around the other and folded his cocked hat into a thousand different shapes"'.[23] Against today's too-slick, soundbite performance-politics, Price's origami, practised on wig, hat and his very body, bespeaks a passionate *living* of the issues and the need to mould and sculpt them into equitable and sustainable forms of being we can all, with dignity, live by.

Damian Walford Davies

Notes

1. See Carl B. Cone, *Torchbearer of Freedom: The Influence of Richard Price on Eighteenth-century Thought* (Lexington, KY: University of Kentucky Press, 1952), 185, 197. Other titles by which Price was known include 'The Apostle of Liberty' and 'The Friend of Mankind'.

2. Richard Price, *Political Writings*, ed. D. O. Thomas (Cambridge: Cambridge University Press, 1991), xv.

3. Cone, *Torchbearer of Freedom*, 197.

4. Lyndall Gordon, *Vindication: A Life of Mary Wollstonecraft* (London: Virago, 2005), 119.

5. Price, *Political Writings*, 39.

6. Ibid., 150. We need to acknowledge, as Anthony Page notes, that Price had a 'low profile' as an abolitionist. While the strength of his opposition to slavery is unambiguous, and the advice given to America crystal clear, it is also plain that he was 'a high-profile metropolitan Rational Dissenter associating with many people connected to the West India trade', whose focus in his last years was firmly on 'the national campaigns for religious and political liberty' rather than explicitly on race and the obscenity of chattel slavery and the slave trade. For Price, of course, securing religious and civil liberty would signal the end of the conditions and imperialist mindset that permitted slavery to exist. However, in this regard, Price 'provides further evidence of how antislavery thought did not translate easily into abolitionist action'. Page again: 'there was an inherent tension between Richard Price's radical language of liberty and his more conventional social views'. See Anthony Page, '"A Species of Slavery": Richard Price's Rational Dissent and Antislavery', *Slavery & Abolition*, 32:1 (2011), 53–73.

7. Paul Frame, *Liberty's Apostle: Richard Price – His Life and Times* (Cardiff: University of Wales Press, 2015), 86.

8. Gordon, *Vindication*, 48.

9. Price, *Political Writings*, 195–6.

10. See ibid., 185 and 190.

11. Edmund Burke, *Reflections on the Revolution in France* (London: J. Dodsley, 1790), 45.

12. Ibid., 13.

13. Richard Price, *A Discourse on the Love of Our Country* (Oxford: Woodstock Books, 1992 [1789]), v.

14. Cone, *Torchbearer of Freedom*, 199.

15. Price, *A Discourse,* vi.

16. Paul Frame and Geoffrey W. Powell, '"Our First Concern as Lovers of Our Country Must be to Enlighten It": Richard Price's Response to the French Revolution', in Mary-Ann Constantine and Dafydd Johnston (eds), *'Footsteps of Liberty and Revolt': Essays on Wales and the French Revolution* (Cardiff: University of Wales Press, 2013), 58.

17. Gordon, *Vindication*, 54.

18. Price, *Political Writings*, 178.

19. Frame and Powell, 'Our First Concern', 58.

20. Frame, *Liberty's Apostle*, 249.

21. Rémy Duthille, 'The Right of Resistance in Richard Price and Joseph Priestley', *History of European Ideas*, 44:4 (2018), 426.

22. Price, *A Discourse*, Appendix, 13.

23. Frame, *Liberty's Apostle*, 86.

Acknowledgements

The editors gratefully acknowledge the support of Cardiff University in the production of this volume and thank Kevin Sinnott for permission to use a detail from his painting *Richard Price* (2015) as the cover image and Chris Lloyd for photographing it.

Angela Graham

The Thinker

What if he hadn't?
What if he hadn't bothered?
What if he hadn't bothered
to plunge into the river
to rescue that drowning man?
One desperate loser
(who neglected to think things through) gone
and the river flowing on.

But, since he'd set aside his coat, his hat, his wig
prudently on the riverbank,
there they were, waiting,
when the two men clambered back.

The rescued tells his tale: no funds, no future
and Price puts the dry coat on him,
hands his horse over
and watches it carry this stranger off
toward tomorrows firmly put back
within his reach.

Walking on, sopping, carrying his wig, his hat,
vagabonded, fit for ridicule,
Price finds his way into my heart.

Nothing doused the flames of his desire
for thought in action;
for reason serving silly, glorious flesh.

Mab Jones

Observations on the
Expectations of Lives

I beg leave to submit to your perusal the following observations – Richard Price

: that life is fast, hard, and brief,
with only small lulls of slowness
which widen quickly, swaddling
into depression, duck arse fat
and doughnut-legged, if you let them;

that this is a world of hierarchies:
kings lolling on queens upending
knights squatting on knaves, with
aces hidden up sleeves belonging to
shirts too expensive for you, *mate*;

that 'key-to-the-door' at 21 symbolises
nothing; except perhaps the plastic,
part-time, never-yours nature of
property, turning the soul of you
into a cheap-o, half-alive pot plant;

that the 'increase of mankind' is now
problematic – a *Countdown* conundrum
composed of 8 billion consonants
and all the vowels gone the way of dodos,
golden toads, sea cows, and mammoths;

and that, though this subject's been considered
by others, I feel it necessary to make my addition;
before the inevitable subtraction of self
from all of this and everything; and, in fact,
in spite of it, because – still,

I am sure that the world owes you
so many discoveries; still,
I hope that your happiness will
continually increase. Indeed, it is my sincere wish:
despite the fisting, thrusting, dumbing crush of it all.

Life's brevity is its breath, also,
whispering joy into a collapsing fissure;
and my expectation is that you will hear it;
beyond this necessary summation, it is calling.
And no matter how few your years, you will respond.

Where E = expectation, and F = the effing inevitable:

$$\sum \frac{E}{F} < \binom{\varnothing}{\infty} \text{æ}$$

Rae Howells

To My Daughter, Aged 10

On reading Richard Price's *Observations on the Expectations of Lives* (1769)

it is said that cities were fatal for children,
half of infants dead before their first
I love you.

two-thirds gone before the age of ten. imagine that.
three centuries ago in mortal London
you are already dead, subject
to one peculiar evil or another – plague, or accident,
or unhealthfulness. a cruel cart's wheel,
a bad drink. you are counted on the London bills,
a dissenter perhaps,
and for his calculations, he thanks the light afforded
by their tally of your stopped heart.

this week you have been teaching me to sing the parts
of Llyn y Fan Fach, harmonies of the quiet woman,
held prisoner in a black lake. we have watched blue tits
nesting in the birdbox. you picked me a dandelion,
and wrote a letter to the government about climate change,
your pencil marks scored deep into the paper.
the house would be so quiet.

the demographer in him worried about cities, their poison,
their tendency to subtract, divide,
to pare down the share of life due to a person.
numbers cannot lie. plainly, there is the great town's inability
to balance the books of yearly births and burials.
inevitable as mathematics or death, the result is inescapable:
more people equals less life.

in spite of your beautiful letter, they will build new houses
on the green space behind your bedroom.
he wanted children to reach the age of marriage. to live
in openness, in country parishes.
now you are ten. he'd want to figure it out.
what is your expectation of life?

Abeer Ameer

Worth

They say with all they say and do
   that some lives are worth less than other lives.
That although all people are born equal,
   some are just worth less than others.

It may be how they got here
   that made them worth less –
if they were hungry, soaked to the bone
      in seawater, clearly they are worth less –
worth less than those always well-fed,
      worth less than those who tread upon red carpets.
Those born into iron chains are worth less
     than those wearing gold chains,
   worth less than those fed from silver spoons.

Those who flee barbed wire fences
are worth less than those who pen boundaries.
They are worth less than those who stamp forelocks,
     are worth less than those with keys to castles.
Those who speak tongues from afar
     are worth less than speakers of fairer tongues.
Those with calloused hands are worth less
     than those with soft hands.
Those who walk barefoot are worth less.
Those whose sight has been scarred are worth less.
Those whose minds are pained are worth less.
Those with untamed spines are worth less.
Those outside Flanders Fields are worth less.
Those from the east of the West are worth less.
Those in the West first are worth less.

They say those whose lives are worth less
          shouldn't complain.
They should accept it as their fate, their destiny.

This is life.

Some lives are worth less than other lives.
Some lives are worth less than others.
Some lives are worth less.

Worth less.

Worthless.

Robert Minhinnick

At Karl Marx's Grave

In the opposite cemetery
I find the grave of Queen Victoria's

horse-slaughterer's wife.
Then the graves of the horse-slaughterer's children.

So many horses went to the knacker's yard,
even the black-feathered horse

that pulled Karl Marx's hearse
on March 17, 1883.

But Michael Way died this week,
the police clearing his bedroll from the entrance

to Spar in John Street, Porthcawl.
How often did I step past Michael

maybe offering something from the Spar deli?
Alkie, of course, like the other street people,

and finally renounced by his family.
I saw neighbours take Michael coffee

or cheese rolls. It was summertime
and we thought the world a fine place,

despite all the horses
gone to the knacker's yard,

even the black-feathered horse
that pulled Karl Marx's hearse.

It's the church that raises the funeral costs
and now I stand on the seafront in my town

and it isn't summer any more,
watching Michael Way's ashes

blowing over the promenade,
listening to the wind

saying *I told him so, I told him so*
and what is there to do in these circumstances

but toast Michael's memory
and think about the grave

of Queen Victoria's horse-slaughterer's wife
and the graves of the horse-slaughterer's children

and all the pretty horses
gone to the knacker's yard

and especially the black feathered horse
that pulled Karl Marx's hearse?

Ghost City
for Nazaar

1.

Writer,
haven't you been told
history begins here?

But more profitable
than cocaine,
it was sold

in meaningless fragments
after the museums were looted.
Dirt poor, the farmers

had found this treasure
in the ashes they tilled.
Yet only war allowed

this dispensation,
rarer than rain
in the Sham desert.

2.

Sixty thousand years
in screenshots? I choose
a Neanderthal woman

arranging wild flowers
in her dead child's hair.
Then Nebuchadnezzar's lions

and a dragon, the *mušḫuššu*
staring down Procession Street,
but our cameraman

refusing to film.
Eerily, those creatures reminded me
of scrapyard dogs

we used to see
in Rover Way at Bird Brothers
roaming near the shredder.

3.

Even in Babylon,
Nazaar reasoned, Saddam's spies
were everywhere –

within the mosque of Ali,
around the mudbrick
foundation of Babel.

You may go, he said,
but I have to remain,
as will the spies,

common as cockroaches
in the Ministry of Information.
So I explored instead

the temple rooms –
where gold was a god
demanding worship.

Yes, whether dinars
or dirhams, money
itself was a glutton for prayer.

But in those dark cells for tiny people,
goat bells had become
the only music left in that ghost city.

Kristian Evans

Y Capel ar Werth

But what language do the dead speak
I wonder, turning the pages
of the old family *Beibl*,
and how to break the lock they placed
on our tongues? Who lack all notion
of limit. *Poetic Genius*
is the true Man, and the body
or outward form of Man is derived
from the Poetic Genius.
That if the future self could speak,
all travesty and misery of history's
dross shaken off and translated
into symbol and *sunthema,*
      would it speak flesh-word or forest?
Restoration of that first bliss
      plucked from Adam's very own breast
or all the endless acres fly
      to the promised land in the west?

Phil Cope

Tynton Farm, Llangeinor
Birthplace of Richard Price, 23 February 1723

From your old front door
you could have rolled right down
to Garw's floor, unhindered;
mining in your day
just surface scrapings
for home fires and domestic furnaces
before the coming of the chaos
and the cruelty of coal.

What did this green land teach you:
that clouds negotiate the soft folds of our hills
without argument or controversy;
that the sky, though penned within our valley's contours,
is owned equally by us all;
that spring waters feed flora and fauna without charge or contract,
and, predictable as seasons, always find
the least combative paths to the sea?

Gerry Ray

Tynton

Moonshine
In the horse's eye

My angry father
Prophesied

And though dissent was in my heart
I loved my mother
My sisters too

For beauty is in the number
The probable in the set

And things are meant to happen
Despite the things we do
Freedom on a rocking horse
Bonds in Pudding Lane

The paradox of perfectibility
Immaterial to the soul –

And right and wrong are simple
Intuit to the mind

No sin in being born –
I'll pray for you, my darling

Play cards and hold you tight . . .

Bunhill Fields

The bones of the dead are buried here –
Blake, Defoe and Bunyan too

Interned by railings to keep the living out
and though insured by statistical chance

Gold's no good for ghosts or bones
profiting on loam or dying leaves

Despite the words of assurance
from Dr Richard Price ...

Taz Rahman

Amygdala

Moral Liberty is the power of following, in all circumstances, our sense of right and wrong; or of acting in conformity to our reflecting and moral principles, without being controlled by any contrary principles – Richard Price, *A Review of the Principal Questions in Morals* (1758)

All my Marches accumulate rubble, the rain struggles
in its bid to silence a structure under the temporal lobe,

an almond shapes beneath the uncus, diverse, complex,
comprising 13 nuclei to decode a room with no door.

I wore Yves Klein in a Paris studio for my birthday,
a new blue, darker than Bengal 1859, the indigo skin

of Kader Molla drained of its worthlessness: *to be
worthless is not being entirely devoid of worth,*

but to be worth less than what is being compared to.
My heart keels in need, a house weans itself off guilt

pretending it is the *waun*, the Biafra embroider pine
for the land swallowed, limpets periwinkle erosion,

venerate wells, make up tales of saints snorkelling
the Atlantic as black grouse. I have held on to a post-it

note once sticky, pretty, I save it for a day that never
comes to write my manifesto on the right of men

to lie on broken futons. The noxious sprouts ladders
for a fallen sapling in the garden where flowers have

forgotten the basics of shredding an unwritten
song in mini-bar ink for a 4th of July. I syncopate

Charles Lloyd scraping cantos through the shared
earphone and America is born so Terrance Hayes

can *carry a flag bearing a different nation on each*
side. In the city of Jahangir, four hundred years

in bodies lean out, face the subtropical afternoon
flame, a lone peanut seller sinks an orange sun

above Hatkhola on his top of the voice *rakben*
badam. I unravel in the folds of a sari, a horse

on a boat pops out the same size inside a glass jar
seen at four, compiles the red list of birds I shall

never see again, my perished father spinning muslin
mutters *what price is independence* when the *tokai*

foliates lyres in original sin, digs for congealed
bhat in the municipal waste, how Paul Simon

carries real estate America for Cathy in his pocket
on a bus ticket to Saginaw. Lambs graze a world

I once liked. I've given up on virtue or the unitary
nature of god as the universal creator of dynamics

phrasing a yelp through streets impersonating
the bloated demolition of an illicit underpass.

Notes

Kader Molla: one of the leaders of the 1859 Nil Bidroho (Indigo Revolt) in
Bengal when rice farmers refused to cultivate indigo instead of food crops and
defied the East India Company rulers

waun: Welsh − moorland

rakben badam: Bengali − 'Would you like to buy peanuts?'

tokai: an impoverished child looking for food or potentially sellable items in open
municipal bins in Bangladesh. The root of the word means 'to collect' in Bengali

bhat: rice

Zoë Brigley

Mary Wollstonecraft at Newington Green Unitarian Chapel

It is certain that no animal brings forth its young with as much difficulty, pain and danger as a woman – Joseph Clark to Richard Price, 9 June 1785

She won't recall the itch of lace at her collar, how
her behind ached on the hard pew, only Price
speaking: this is happiness, such beginnings, his
attention to her, a man thin and modest, rider
of a half-blind horse, dressed in black with sympathy
for birds and women. In his defence, she'll write:
The world is not yet civilized enough. From Price,
she learns that liberty is deciding for oneself –
but death shows the limits of women's freedom:
missed by her doctor, the placenta curdling
the womb will kill her before she can know
her newborn. So much for self-determination.
Still, the arched windows are full of light as
Price says: *You cannot hold the world in darkness.*

Mari Ellis Dunning

Mary Wollstonecraft Speaks
of Richard Price

When we first met, I thought him like a sparrow –
he was rail-thin, narrow as a rachis, two feathery plumes
angling his brow. But his coat wrapped him
like crow's wings, stiff and black.
When he spoke, his voice was birdsong, syrupy
and light. A new dawn. I leaned forward
in the pulpit, drank the words in. Felt
them resonate in my own heaving chest.
He didn't flinch when I said young girls
should feel each blade of grass needling
between their toes, should scramble
tree trunks and nestle in branches.
I pictured them running free as does.
Instead, he spoke of torch-bearing,
of handing flames to our children
before our own sparks diminished. He spoke
of countries oceans away, of revolution,
of vast green openness. He spoke
of dismantling crowns, told me
to carry my own sceptre. Later, I remembered
what I could of his sermons, spilled the words
like milk straight from my mouth. I penned
my own vindications – wrote of girls
and women harnessing their power
like herbs from the ground.
Like me, he gathered his strength
from the wind, let each gust bolster him
so that suddenly I saw him as a red kite.
I saw him sweeping nations.

Richard Marggraf Turley

The Spy

Gillray's cartoon, *Copenhagen Fields* (1795)

That's me, tucked between tanner and tailor,
candlestick maker. A pair of eyes
beneath a hat, below the speaker's cuffed fist.
A confidential face? The artist knew
to hedge the phiz.
      It's the gagging air
I most remember, stifling the call to order.
Then, from the rostrum, the *Whoomph!*
of that raggy umbrella.
Some gurning
fool – whose name I can supply –
cracked its ribs, held it as a coffered fly-loft,
framing our likely lad, who took the stand
to tatty cheers.
      His was a practised play
of voice and pose, though *dilettantish*, sir.
Yes, I egged him on, lent his brawling speech
an abetting tongue.
      How he punched! –
conducting discord with that mercer's
paw.
      I moved nimbly in the aftershock,
traded nods with citizen Bone.
My mark? Not the man himself,
but two budding poets poised in the outfield,
perched on that branch of Tyburn's Tree.

Damian Walford Davies

Dr Price at Southerndown*
1790

You wouldn't call it bathing,
not that last July. Still, he braved
the revolutions of the chill
Welsh tides in moleskin long johns,
parlour slippers shod with cork

against the razor shells. He'd scruffle
out across the blue republics
of the mussel beds until
the water soothed his gothic
knee and bladderwrack lapped

slick against his bladder stones.
He knew the limits: riptides
that could carry you to France;
sandbanks sheering plumb
to depths where congers cruise

as kings; blooms of jellyfish
that burn red lashes on the back.
The offing had the blankness
of an empty meeting house, bright
lines of surf like lacquered pews.

In his dressing gown he'd take
a census of the rockpools,
tallying the waving populations
and the swift, translucent lives.
Above, the cliff's blue lias

rose in layers, uncut pages
of a book, ammonites like grim
cathedral bosses spinning
in the rock. That last July, before
his pony led him up the hill,

his dentures crunching grains
of sand, he watched a warship
hoist its ensign under Exmoor,
stood there thin and wigless –
harmless and seditious, facing west.

* Richard Price was a committed sea bather throughout
his life, taking to the water during annual breaks in
Brighton and Eastbourne and at Southerndown
(Dunraven Bay) in his native Glamorgan.

Hilary Watson

Alternative Beginning

Suppose, in the beginning there was uncertainty
and it was good. And we taught our children that.
Acceptance, felt deep within; the vagus nerve
wandering the body, carrying with it acceptance.
The trinity of body, mind, spirit not spliced to three,
staying as one. Suppose, at the start we celebrated
the darkness as much as the light, found ways
of communing and conversing even when the odds
of winning were stacked against us. And shame became
a true synonym of sorrow on the heart, not a baptism
of not good, not enough. Suppose, the pain we bore
was felt, felt out and left to rise. Let there be progress
at the speed of evolutionary anatomy, and threats
proportional to the task with no sceptre of sabretooth.

ChatGPT

What is your favourite childhood memory?
I have many fond memories from my childhood, but one that stands out is when I learned how to ride a bike without training wheels.

How do you like to spend your weekends?
I enjoy spending time outdoors, exploring new places, and trying new activities. I also like to relax and unwind by reading a good book or watching a movie.

If you could have any superpower, what would it be and why?
I think it would be cool to have the power of teleportation, so I could instantly travel to any location in the world without having to deal with the hassle of transportation.

What is your favourite book and why?
My favourite book is *To Kill a Mockingbird* by Harper Lee because of its powerful message about social justice and its memorable characters.

Do you prefer cats or dogs?
I like both cats and dogs, but I would say I prefer dogs because of their loyalty and affectionate nature.

What is your favourite type of food?
I enjoy a wide variety of foods, but I particularly like spicy cuisine such as Thai or Indian food.

If you could travel to any place in the world, where would you go and why?
I would love to travel to Japan because of its unique culture, beautiful scenery, and delicious food.

What do you think is the biggest problem facing society today?
I believe one of the biggest problems facing society today is the increasing polarisation and division among different groups of people, which can lead to hostility and conflict.

If you had a time machine, what era would you visit and why?
I would like to visit the Renaissance era in Europe, as it was a time of great artistic and intellectual achievement and would be fascinating to experience firsthand.

If you could speak to Dr Richard Price, what would you say?
I would ask Dr Richard Price about his experiences and insights as a philosopher and mathematician, and how he views the intersection of these two fields. Additionally, I would be curious to learn about his perspective on the implications of artificial intelligence for philosophy and society as a whole.

Kevin Mills

Dr Price Versus UFOs

The three best-known UFO stories from Wales concern incidents in the Berwyn mountains (1974), Broad Haven (1977) and Pentyrch (2016).

Richard Price's words are taken from *Four Dissertations*, IV: 'On the Importance of Christianity, The Nature of Historical Evidence, and Miracles' (1767).

1. Probabilities

Suppose the flowing of the tide,
    (maybe that day in Broad Haven)
if it has flowed,
    (when light split into silver)
at the end of a certain interval,
    (and phosphor over the school)
a million of times,
    (early Feb   was the point)
there would be the probability,
    (of no return)
expressed by .5105, that the odds for its
    (saucer-eyed kids drew)
flowing again,
    (the craft   the Head incredulous)
at the usual period,
    (end of the day I was out there)
was greater than 1,400,000 to one,
    (peeking through trees)
and the probability expressed by .5352
    (at faceless humanoids)
that the odds was less than 1,600,000 to one.

Such are the conclusions which
uniform experience warrants.

2. Testimonies

Let us consider what is
   (flying in our airspace)
the ground of the regard we pay
   (orbs, triangles, discs, cigars)
to human testimony. We may,
   (see here blurred and winking)
I think, see plainly,
   (on my phone before it)
that it is not experience only
   (died)
meaning, all along, that kind of experience
   (the light split into three)
to which we owe our expectation
   (above Pentyrch trees left)
of natural events, the causes of which are unknown
   (snapped mid-trunk white)
to us. Were this the case, the
   (scorch marks all long the cut)
regard we ought to pay to testimony,
   (figures then in hazmat)
would be in proportion to the number of
   (suits scoured the ground)
instances, in which we have found,
   (*we have to find it* heard repeatedly)
that it has given us right information, compared
   (Geiger clicked a hail)
with those in which it has deceived us;
   (and all we got were denials)
and it might be calculated in the same manner
   (cover stories FoI exemptions)
with the regard due to any conclusions
   (anomalies persist as does official silence)
derived from induction.

But this is by no means
the truth.

3. Accounts

One cannot help being greatly disgusted
  (on Berwyn mountain)
with the inclination which shews itself in
  (those who felt it knew)
many persons, to treat with contempt
  (the Richter scale was needed)
whatever they hear,
  (aircraft down earthquake asteroid)
be it ever so well attested, if
  (I saw light split coals come down)
it happens that they are not able to account for
  (the valley aglow red yellow white)
it, or that it does not coincide with
  (a shape loaded onto a truck)
 their experience, just as if they knew
  (in the dark)
all that can take place in nature, or
  (I heard *three* official stories)
as if their experience was
  (I saw what I saw)

the standard of truth and
measure of possibility.

Tracey Rhys

Before the Book of John there was the Word

. . . I often wonder what the world would be, had he left it at that.
Had none of them that followed – Luke, Matthew or Mark –
picked up a quill, presented Him like some elaborate choice
played out for fear. This life's a game, a *Jumanji*, or a *Risk*,
beginner's chess or skint *Monopoly*. And no one's born with sin
or even hope, or thoughts other than *feed me, love me*.
God knows, innocence must come before the teat,
and longer still before the knowledge forms.
And how it floods our little phones today.
This life is full of words and pictures now.

Contributors

Abeer Ameer's poems have appeared widely in journals including *The Rialto, The Poetry Review, Under the Radar* and *Poetry Wales*. Her debut poetry collection, *Inhale/Exile*, in which she shares stories of her Iraqi forebears, was published by Seren in 2021 and shortlisted for Wales Book of the Year in 2022.

Zoë Brigley is the author of three poetry collections from Bloodaxe, all PBS Recommendations, most recently *Hand & Skull* (2019). She is editor of *Poetry Wales* and joint poetry editor at Seren Books.

Phil Cope is a writer and photographer who lives in Richard Price's birth valley, the Garw. His publications include works exploring Haitian vodou, the Spanish Civil War, Paul Robeson, and the Olympic and Paralympic Games, as well as five major volumes on sacred springs and holy wells. He is currently working on a book of poetry and photographs inspired by worldwide well-spring sites.

Mari Ellis Dunning's debut poetry collection, *Salacia*, was shortlisted for Wales Book of the Year 2019. Her second collection, *Pearl and Bone*, was voted *Wales Arts Review*'s Number 1 Poetry Choice of 2022. Mari is a PhD candidate at Aberystwyth University, where she is writing a historical novel about the 16th-century witch trials in Wales.

Kristian Evans is a poet, editor and environmental activist from Bridgend. He co-edited *100 Poems to Save the Earth* (Seren), and is founding editor of *Modron*, an online magazine of writing about the ecological crisis. He writes a regular column, *A Kenfig Journal*, for the charity Sustainable Wales/Cymru Gynaliadwy.

Angela Graham is from Belfast and lives in Northern Ireland and Wales. Seren Books published her poetry collection, *Sanctuary: There Must Be Somewhere*, in 2022 and her short story collection, *A City Burning* (longlisted for the Edge Hill Short Story Prize), in 2020. She is an award-winning TV and film producer.

Rae Howells is a poet, journalist and lavender farmer. Her debut collection, *The Language of Bees* (Parthian), was shortlisted for Wales Book of the Year 2023. She is a *Rialto* poetry competition winner and her work has featured in journals including *Magma, The Rialto, Poetry Wales* and *Poetry Ireland*. www.raehowells.co.uk

Mab Jones is the author of three collections and three pamphlets, is the recipient of many awards, has presented several BBC Radio 4 programmes, and has written for the *New York Times*. Her latest book is *Yubitsume* (2022), published by Indigo Dreams.

Richard Marggraf Turley won the 2007 Keats-Shelley Prize for Poetry and is author of the collection *Wan-Hu's Flying Chair* (Salt, 2009), which won the 2013 Wales Book of the Year 'People's Choice' award. He teaches in the Department of English and Creative Writing at Aberystwyth University.

Kevin Mills is Professor of English Literature at University of South Wales. He has published three poetry collections, three monographs and many essays and chapters on literary topics. A study of myth and ancient narratives will appear in 2024 from Bloomsbury. He is currently working on a collection of ballads and songs.

Robert Minhinnick published *Menhenet* (Clutag) and *Wild Swimming at Scarweather Sands* (Black Spring) in 2023. He organises the 'Green Room' series of events for the charity Sustainable Wales/Cymru Gynaliadwy in Porthcawl. In 2024, these will feature sessions on 'politics' and 'art'.

Taz Rahman's first poetry collection, *East of the Sun, West of the Moon*, is forthcoming in February 2024 from Seren Books. He was part of the Hay Festival 'Writers at Work' development programme, was shortlisted for the 2022 Aesthetica Creative Writing Prize, and was part of the 2021 Literature Wales annual writer development scheme. He has been published in a number of poetry magazines including *Poetry Wales*.

Gerry Ray has published regularly with *Seventh Quarry* magazine. He often performs in the 'Green Room', Porthcawl at events organised by Sustainable Wales/Cymru Gynaliadwy. Born in Cardiff, he studied English at Nottingham University and later lectured at the Institute of Health Care Studies, Cardiff.

Tracey Rhys is a Welsh writer, artist and editor. Her poetry and short stories can be found in numerous anthologies and journals. Poems from her collection, *Teaching a Bird to Sing*, featured as monologues in two new theatre productions and in word-and-image exhibitions across Wales, including at the Senedd. She won the Poetry Archive's 'WordView Now!' competition in 2020.

Damian Walford Davies is Deputy Vice-Chancellor at Cardiff University. His poetry collections include *Suit of Lights* (2009), *Witch* (2012), *Judas* (2015), *Docklands* (2019) and *Viva Bartali!* (2023), all published by Seren. His academic work focuses on the relation between literature and political culture in the Romantic period.

Hilary Watson is from South Wales. She studied at the University of Warwick and was a Jerwood/Arvon Mentee. Her poems have appeared in *Poetry Wales*, *Magma* and *Poetry Birmingham*. She was shortlisted for the Live Canon Prize 2022 and commended in the York Poetry Prize 2021. @poetryhilary. Hilarywatson.co.uk